# HOW CHRISTMAS CAME TO BE- WITH MOLLY AND ME!!

Written and Illustrated
by Candy A. Johansen

Copyright © 2017 Candy A. Johansen

Photography by Candy A. Johansen

All Rights Reserved.

No Reproduction of this book, complete or partial

may be used, reproduced or transmitted in any form

or means without written permission from the author.

# DEDICATION PAGE

I want to dedicate this book to my mom, who loves Christmas. She has always made Christmas a wonderful and happy time for all of her children, and yet has managed to teach us the true meaning of Christmas and taught us to love God before anything else. You're the best!! I love you, mom!!

# THANK YOU PAGE

Mom and I (Molly) want to thank Hobby Lobby, and Home Depot for letting us come into your stores and photograph. You were wonderful to us. We also want to thank Aunt Pat for helping us find all the Christmas items we needed for our photos. Thank you Grandma Bev and Connie Bent for the use of your houses and porch. And, all of our friends and family, who not only support us, but encourage us in our journey.

## About Molly

Molly is a four-year old pug that lives in Kansas. Molly stays busy as she helps her mom create these books. Her favorite thing to do is go to schools, libraries, and daycares and visit with the children after her mom reads Molly's books to them. When she's not working with her mom, she loves to go for walks at the park, eat her favorite treats, take baths, and play with her sister, Dolly.

The first recorded Christmas was a long time ago-
in 336 while Constantine was the Roman
Emperor.  A few years after that, Pope Julius I
decided that the birth of Jesus would be celebrated
on December 25th.
The name "Christmas" comes from the Mass of
Christ. A mass (or communion) service is where
Christians remember that Jesus died for us and
was raised from the dead.
So, the word "Christmas" comes from the
word, "Christ -Mass."

No one knows the real birthday of Jesus, but Christmas is celebrated on December 25th around the world. It's a time when families come together and a time of giving. Remember... when you celebrate Christmas, you are celebrating a real event that took place about 2000 years ago when God sent his son into the world.

And, that's how Christmas came to be. Join me (Molly) as I learn more about Christmas and why we use certain items to decorate.

When the weather started getting cold, I saw people putting up pretty lights and decorations. I heard people talk about Christmas and presents and Santa Claus. I didn't know what it all meant. Do you understand what Christmas is?

My mom saw me watching her and saw my puzzled
look. She knew I didn't understand. She snuggled
on the couch with me one night after putting up some
Christmas decorations and told me why we celebrate
Christmas. You need to hear this too!! Here's what
she said:

Christmas is a time for people to be happy. Christmas is Jesus' birthday and that's why we celebrate it. When is your birthday?

When Jesus was born, he brought lots of happiness and hope into the world.

Is your family happy when you celebrate your birthday? Do you have a party? Are you happy when it's your birthday?

All the things we see and decorate with at

Christmas have special meanings.

Do you have a toy that is special to you? This

is my favorite toy.

We see angels at Christmas. Angels bring
messages from God. Angels told Jesus' mother
Mary, that she was going to have a special baby for
God. His name would be Jesus.
After Jesus was born, angels also told the shepherds
who were watching their sheep in the hills, about
his birth.

We see stars at Christmas time. A really bright star in the sky on the first Christmas showed three wise men where to go and find baby Jesus. Have you ever looked up in the sky and saw a bright star? Our mom's and dad's put stars on top of our Christmas trees. Does your tree have a star on it?

We see lots of people giving gifts at Christmas time. People give gifts because God gave us a gift- his son, baby Jesus. After Jesus was born, three wise men brought some very special gifts and gave them to baby Jesus because they knew he was a special gift. Do you like getting gifts? Do you remember a special gift someone gave to you? Maybe you can make someone else a special gift for Christmas.

We see mangers during the Christmas season. Do you know what a manger is? A manger was a box that held the animals food. Jesus was laid in a manger after he was born because there was no room in the inn. Jesus was not born in a hospital like most babies. He was born in a small outdoor building called a stable. Animals, like sheep and cows were kept in a stable.

We see and hear bells at Christmas time- all kinds of bells. We ring bells at Christmas time to symbolize the joy of Christmas and to announce and celebrate the birth of Jesus. How many different places do you hear bells ringing during Christmas?

We see candlelight at Christmas time. We light candles to show that Jesus is the light of the world and his light guides us to do what is right. Do you have candles in your house?

We see candy canes during Christmas. A long time ago, sheperds used a long stick called a "shepherds crook" to protect their sheep and candy canes are shaped like the crook. Also, the candy cane looks like the letter "J" which stands for Jesus.

Do you eat candy canes during Christmas? Or, do you help your family decorate your Christmas tree with them?

We see Santa Claus during the Christmas season. Santa is a gift from God to make children happy at Christmas. He brings us toys to play with. You sit on his lap and tell him what you want for Christmas. We sit out cookies for him to eat when he comes to deliver toys. We watch for him in the sky with his reindeer. Have you ever sat on Santa's lap?

During the Christmas season, we see pinecones. Sometimes, they are hanging on a wreath and sometimes, they are just sitting in a basket. Pinecones represent good health and protection. Do you have any pinecones in your home?

We see Christmas trees during the Christmas season- in homes, in stores, in churches... everywhere. We use evergreen trees as Christmas trees because they will not die, fade away or lose their needles in the winter time. It stands for a sign of hope throughout the winter season- hope that the rest of nature will also awaken to life coming in the spring. Christmas trees also represent the hope that we have in Jesus Christ.

At Christmas time, we see and hear a lot about reindeer... pulling Santa's sleigh. Reindeer means a "horned animal" or a "running animal." Did you know that both the male and female reindeer grow horns? Does your dad hunt? Ask him if female deer have horns too.

Also, reindeer are fast runners. They can run up to sixty miles per hour. That's as fast as your car. Reindeer are also very sure-footed. They won't slip on ice or snow. God gave the reindeer unique gifts just like he gave you and me and he wants us to use those gifts.

We see snowmen during the Christmas season. We sometimes build a snowman in the winter when it snows. Christmas is in December, which is one of the cold months of winter. Have you ever built a snowman? In the song, "Frosty the Snowman," Frosty puts a hat on his head and then "begins to dance around." That's the way we do when we are little. As soon as we can walk, we are out running around experiencing the world. We laugh, we play, we run and we explore. That's the way Jesus was when he was a child too. Even though Jesus knew he was God's son, he lived his life as a child just like me and you.

We see lots of Christmas lights during the Christmas season. A long time ago, candles were used instead of Christmas lights. The Christmas lights symbolize Christ, who is the light of the world, and we use them to remind us to provide light to other people, not only at Christmas time, but every day.

We see wreaths hanging everywhere at Christmas time. Sometimes they are decorated with lights and Christmas balls and sometimes, they have holly and ivy on them. Wreaths are round and the roundness means that life always continues, just like a circle has no end. Do you have a wreath hanging in your house?

We see poinsettia's at Christmas time. Churches are usually decorated with poinsettia's during the Christmas season. This is what a poinsettia looks like. The plant means, "Star Flower." A long time ago, the top of the poinsettia was used as a dye for skin and clothes. Do you have a red shirt? The color could've come from a poinsettia. This plant can grow big and tall if planted after Christmas.  Remind your mom to plant it in a pot... and then watch it grow.

We see mistletoe hanging up at Christmas. This is a picture of it. Have you ever see mistletoe? When your mom or dad hang mistletoe in your house, it is supposed to bring good luck to your household.

Have you ever seen your mom and dad kiss under the mistletoe at Christmas? A long time ago, mistletoe was used as a sign of love and friendship and that's why people give kisses under a mistletoe. When your parents kiss under the mistletoe, it is simply a sign that they love each other.

During the Christmas season, we see holly and ivy. Holly are the red berries and they represent good health, faith in God and happiness and joy. Does Christmas make you happy? The holly leaves remind us of the crown of thorns that Jesus wore and the red berries are the color of his blood. During Christmas, we also see ivy. Ivy is the green plant. This plant reminds us that even when life gets tough, we are supposed to trust in God and keep growing.

We see Nativity sets at Christmas time.

A Nativity set is showing us what it was like when Jesus was born. You'll see Mary (Jesus' mother), Joseph (Jesus' daddy on earth), baby Jesus lying in a manger, cows, sheep and maybe even a donkey. Have you ever seen a Nativity set?

We see and notice snowflakes more at Christmas
time. Why? Because Christmas comes just a few days
after the winter season begins and snow most often
falls during this time of year. Have you ever caught
a snowflake with your tongue? Or, looked at one very
closely? Snowflakes usually have six sides and God
creates each snowflake unique, just like he created
you and me. God not only cares about the big things-
he also cares about the little things... like snowflakes.

At Christmas time and during the winter months, we see alot of sleds. A sled has two runners on the bottom side of it to make it slide easily across a surface. Sleds are mostly used on snow or ice. A long time ago, when sleds were first invented, they were used to haul heavy objects. Today, we see large sleds that carry people or goods that are pulled by horses or dogs. We mostly see small sleds as children are sledding on snow in the winter time. And, around Christmas time, we always think of Santa riding in his sleigh (or sled) as he brings toys around to children.

We see turtle doves at Christmas time. Sometimes, they are used as Christmas tree decorations. Doves are a Christmas symbol because the bible talks about them as being loyal and loving.

Doves are also symbols of peace. We use doves at Christmas so we can remember that Jesus was born into the world to bring peace between God and man.

We see Wise men at Christmas time. Wise men are celebrate Jesus' birth and wise men came to bring Jesus gifts after he was born. The wise men gave Jesus three gifts: gold, frankincense, and myrrh. Do you remember seeing Wise men in a nativity set? What are they typically wearing? How do you know they are wise men?

And... that's the reason we celebrate Christmas. I hope you've enjoyed learning why we use the different Christmas decorations and what they mean. I've had a ton of fun with mom creating this book for you.

MERRY CHRISTMAS!!!

www.ingramcontent.com/pod-product-compliance
Lightning Source LLC
Chambersburg PA
CBHW042132070426
42453CB00002BA/14